where flowers bloom

Copyright © 2020 Brianna Rae Quinn

All rights reserved, No portion of this book may be reproduced in any form without permission from the publisher, except as permitted by U.S. copyright law. For permissions contact:

miss.briannaquinn@gmail.com

Cover Art by Brianna Rae Quinn

ISBN: 978-1-7356362-0-7
eISBN: 978-1-7356362-1-4

*This book is dedicated to
any little girl who has been told
she can't.*

"Where flowers bloom,

        so does hope."

                -Lady Bird Johnson

Table of Contents

I am...

NOSTALGIC	1
EMPTY	9
ALONE	16
INSPIRED	23
CREATIVE	30
PASSIONATE	37
POWERFUL	44
JEALOUS	51
FOOLISH	58
AFRAID	65
MISUNDERSTOOD	73
DEJECTED	80
UNCERTAIN	88
CONFIDENT	94
FORGIVING	101
ASHAMED	108
HOPEFUL	115
COURAGEOUS	122
TIRED	129
AMBITIOUS	136
PROUD	143
AT PEACE	150
THANKFUL	157

I am...
NOSTALGIC
the pansy

The Box in the Closet

I've come across the pink,
hardbound, composition notebook
Many times over the years.
It belonged to a little girl,
Who, more than anything, loved to write.

She filled pages with chicken scratch
resembling rhyming words and stories.
This was her journal, and
She wished one day she could be
A real author,

She'd spend hours on her floor,
Writing poems, songs,
plays, and stories, and
Drawing pictures until her
Little hands cramped up,

Brianna Rae Quinn

Stacking the pages and
Stapling the bindings,
Placing them neatly in a
Blue paper folder which she kept
On her at all times.

And even in the silliest tales
The words are filled with her
Passion and her pride, and I
Wonder how she'd feel seeing
Them boxed up in a dusty, closet corner.

Perhaps it's time I take
A page from her book,
And honor her wish, and her ambition.
She's always been an author,
And now I'm going to prove it.

I Adore my Purple Heels
What do I like?
I like my ponytail on the top of my head.
I like my shirts inside out
And my pants hemmed at two different lengths.

I love it when my eye makeup reaches beyond my brows,
and my blush extends to my ears.
The clasp on my necklace is always between my collarbones
Because I like it that way.

I adore my purple heels that hardly fit,
And my orange jeans that match them perfectly.
I love these things because they're me.
I don't see the problem.

(2009)

I am Alice
I look into your eyes, and
Almost instantly, I'm swallowed up.
I am welcomed by my escape,
My Wonderland.

I am lost,
With nowhere to go.
I only fall
d
  e
    e
      p
        e
          r
As I find the center.

A mushroom lay at the bottom,
And I choose
One side to chew.
Then I grow.

I occupy much of the space
When I stay in Wonderland.
Is there room
For the Queen?

I wish I could stay longer;
I always do.
My wonderland is safe.
Usually.

Until there is a day
When I choose the wrong side of the mushroom,
I come and go as I please,
Never forced to leave.

I happily stay, because
I am Alice,
The innocent but mischievous little girl,
Lost in all of Wonderland.

Longing for Sunlight

How can I
Long for sunlight
When the stars
Are so much
More beautiful
Against the vast
Navy skies?

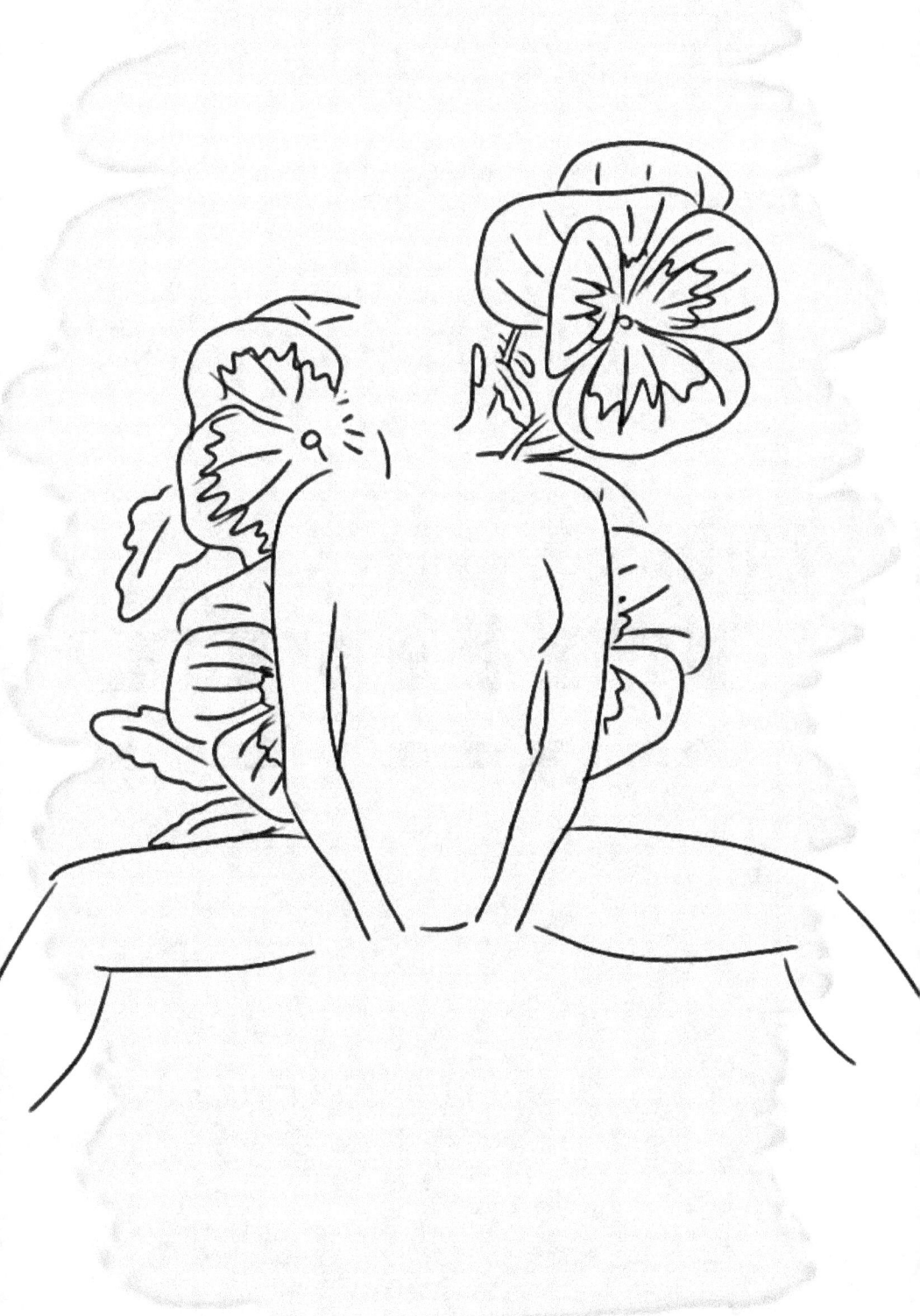

I am...
EMPTY
the vines

Desert

Rolling dunes
And hills of sand
Reflecting heat
Back into the sun.
Sliding mirages
Across the sky
Until the line of
Horizons blurred
Beyond recognition.

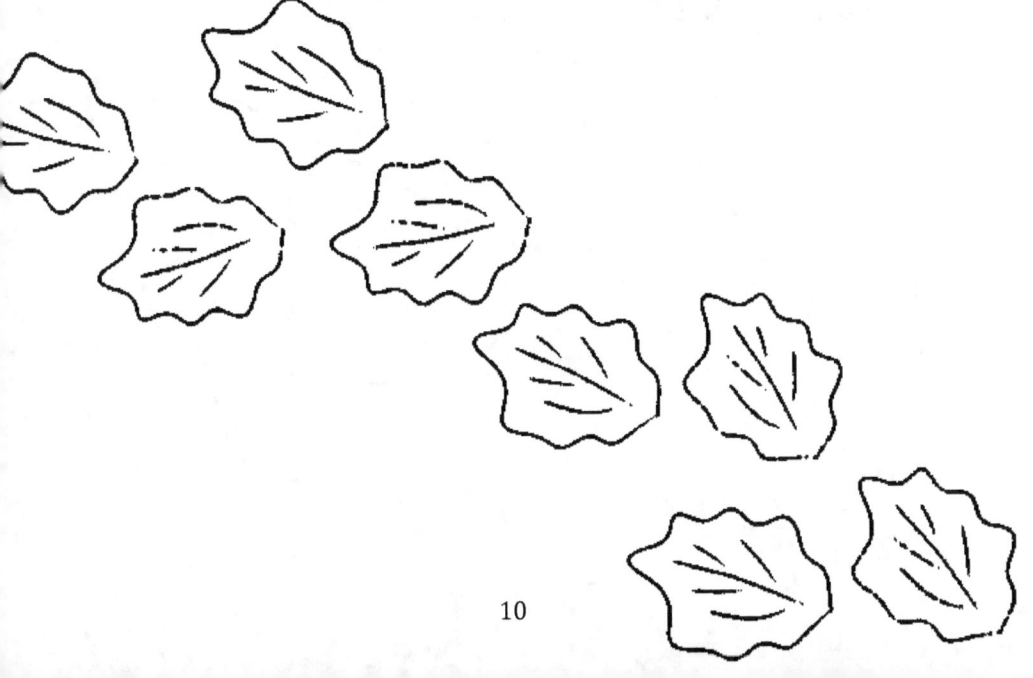

Dried

a flower,

wilts

if

They

leave

It

(2010)

The Act

I wash my face;
I stare in the mirror,
Decorated in darkened circles
And dulled, grey eyes.

So, I assemble a mask
over ivory skin,
Blackening eyelashes,
Painting in lost color.

Blistering heat behind the ears,
Contorting to a playful bounce.
Until I become
Something.

I stand up straight,
And tomorrow,
I'll wake up
And try again.

(2012)

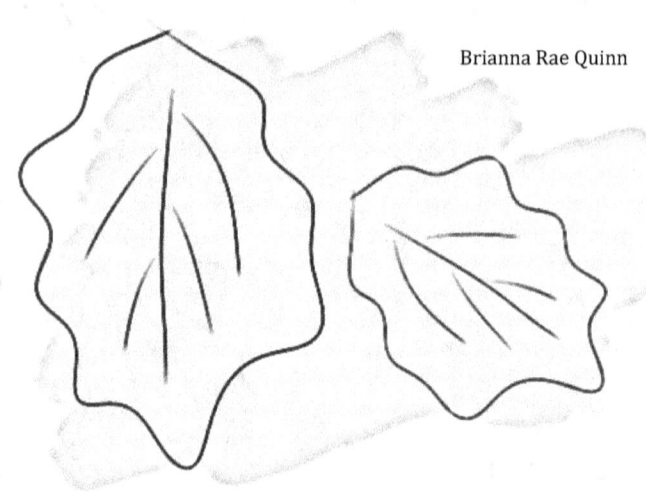

Brianna Rae Quinn

Space
I couldn't be stopped
Until there was nothing left.

April 30th
Colors began to
Fade yesterday. I wonder
What made them do that.

(2012)

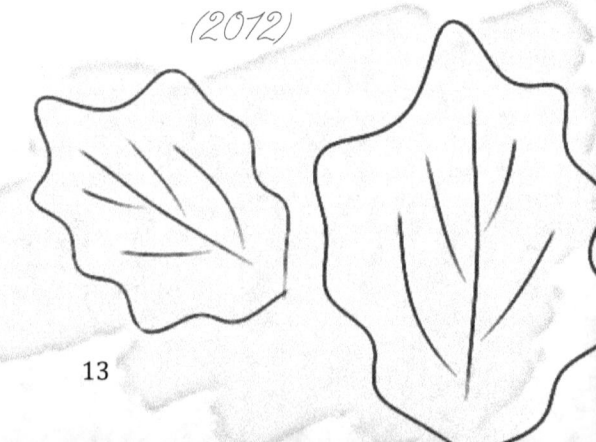

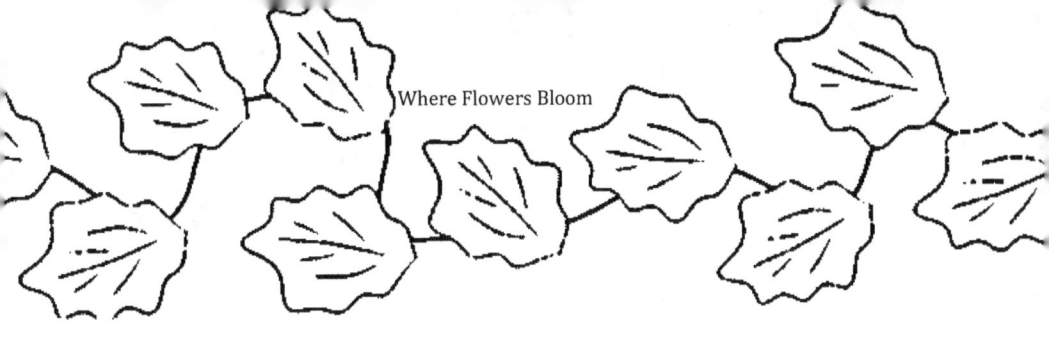

Uninhabited
Umbrosous and
Nefarious, the brain
Intimidates the
Nobody
Housed inside its
Angular walls,
Barring any
Impression of
Temptation or
Emotion without
Delay.

I am...
ALONE
the daffodil

No one can hear me

So small, and insignificant,
I fit upon her shoulder, and
I lamented all the chaos around me.
The roll of her eyes, made me rumble,
Before she brushed me off her shoulder
Falling further until I reached
The cool of the table.
"This is just the same as always.
This is nothing new."
I felt that coolness on my
Fingertips before it faded,
Slipping between the
Cracks until
There was no feeling left,
And the conversations
Between the others
Drifted into darkness.
I had called before the echoes
Could drown out the sounds of distant
Words.
No one can hear me....
No one can hear me....
No one can hear me....
No one can hear me....

(2010)

Mispronunciation
Call me by my name.

You don't decide for someone else
Who they are, or what their identify
Gets to be,
Because the difference
Reflects on how I choose to be seen
And my personality.
I want to be seen as I see me,

So call me by my name.

Connotation
When the only eyes
That exist go beyond the
Four walls of these rooms,
I can shift, and shuffle
Through the halls;
I can kick and swirl
Until I grow dizzy from
The turns.

I can write and I can read
In quiet and peace,
And only when I choose to
Have those eyes on me,
I will.

Group Projects

I recall sitting in the center of
The room, when the teacher said,
"Get in pairs!"

And I scanned the room for any
similarly
Lonely eyes to nestle into the desk
beside me.
When the room had settled, and the
teacher again

Began to speak, I chose to stay silent.
I've never been a fan of
Group projects.

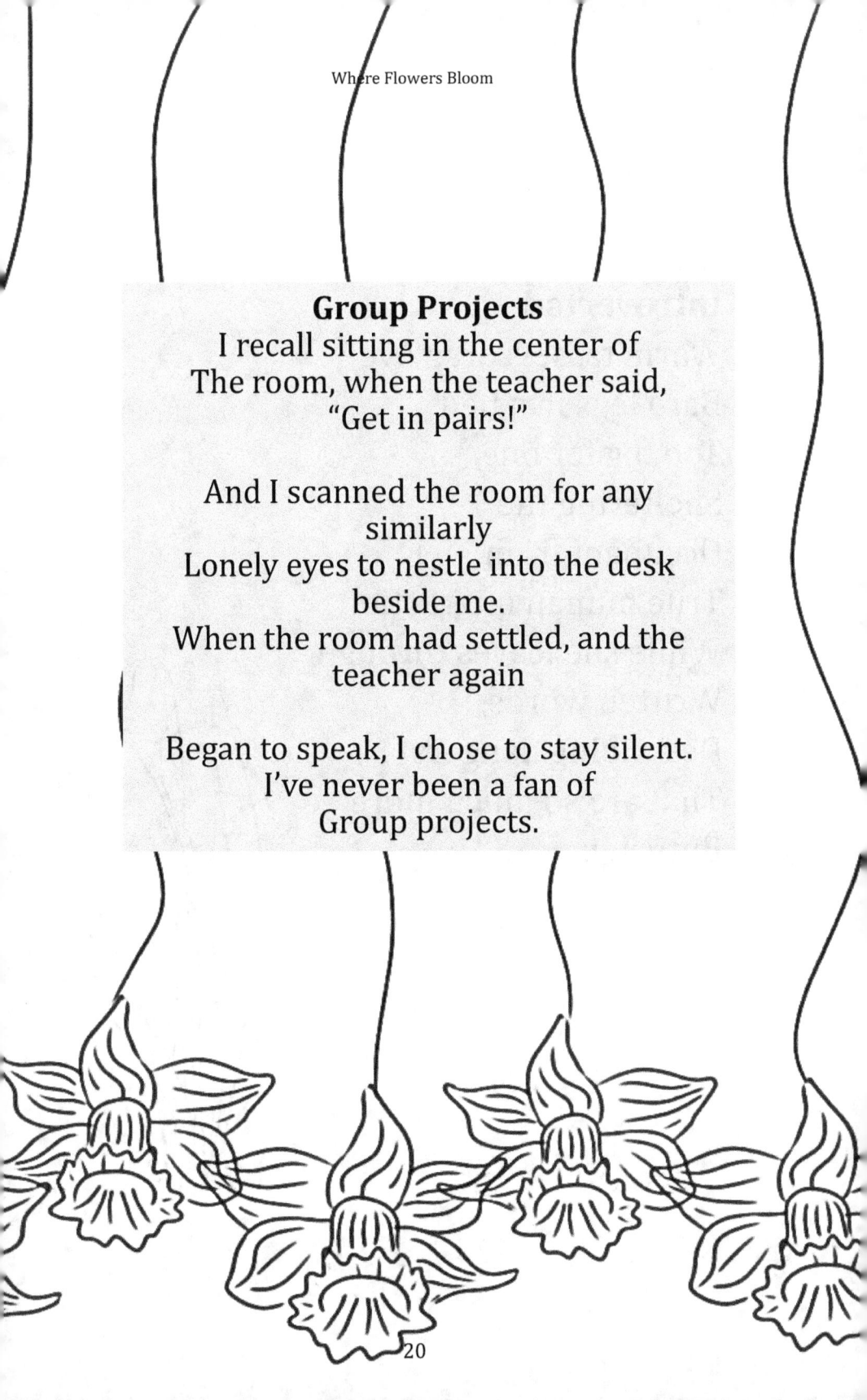

Introverted
Warm tassels drag over
Bare legs in a bed
Too big for one,
Sheltering the
Occupant from
True human interaction
While she leaves through
Written words,
Describing dangers
That are so much more
Enticing.

I am...

INSPIRED
the yarrow

Soul

I remember sitting,
Wishing
Inspiration would come;
I wondered why
Some think it's easy.

My efforts to search
Fail, inevitably
Because I must wait
For it to find me.

(2011)

Success Stories

Every time she
Jumps a hurdle
She makes it look
So easy.

When she dives
Into the pool
She comes out
Looking best.

Now when I come
To a hurdle,
I close my eyes,
And jump

Then even if I miss,
I won't ever
Shy away from
The challenge.

For Me

I used to write about
Places I'd never see,
Things I couldn't feel,
And people I'd never be
Because I thought that's what
People would read.

Now I write mostly
For me.

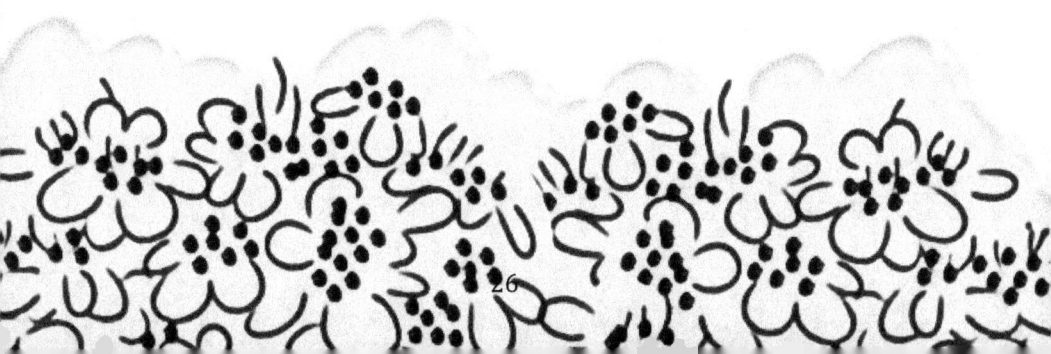

Brianna Rae Quinn

The Pink Hardcover Composition Notebook
I refuse to be
Ashamed of
My silliest
Most immature
Writings,
Because even
The most cliché
Of the bunch
Inspires me
To do better.

Craving Ambition
Human will is not a science.
Salmon have the reputation,
Driven with ambition,
To get upstream every year;
While I sit idle for two straight,
(Or more)
Waiting to find purpose.

I wish I were more like
The salmon.
(2019)

I am...
CREATIVE
the marigold

Brianna Rae Quinn

Sonnet 155

If I were Shakespeare, I'd write on the plight
Of Persephone and her mother's pain;
The prayers of Athens every night,
Desperate to end the harsh snow and rain.
I'd write unnamed sonnets on my dearest
Mistress, and how her morning-breath smells
Just horrid. And though I claim to love her dearly, I don't think
Her lips quite compare to those of the Earl of Southampton.
This is so ridiculous, I'm quitting the
Rhymes and syllable counting. What an awful lot of work for
A nameless poet, and a nameless sonnet. Perhaps I could
Dedicate seven reticent years to hone my skills as well.
If I wrote like Shakespeare, you might know my name.
But truly, iambic pentameter is too damn hard.

(2014)

When Pen Meets Paper

Forget black and white;
We write in color;
We decide the image;
We imagine our own.

Cathartic is the stream of ink
Reflecting our truest self like
The mirror.

Pressure on the pad and
The feeling of friction,
Pushing back into the palm
Of the creator,

Heated and heavy
Forging diamonds.

That Girl

I envy the girl whose eyes open wide as she lies in bed
Before tiptoeing to her desk.
Even in the moonlight, she cannot be stopped.
She drafts and draws until the sunlight comes and goes again
She actualizes her thoughts so consistently, it's almost as if
The thoughts are born through her art.

Meanwhile, I lie awake at night, overflowing with the want.
Yet when I tiptoe to my desk, I idle,
Feeling the resistance through my palms
For the fear my lack of talent
Might make my art unworthy--
Or that those who see
Might disagree.

So tonight, I'll go to bed and close my eyes.
I will rip them open and decide I am worthy.

I will become that girl.

Figures

These words are illustrated
By my finger
Forming symbols
Falling from the feral thoughts
Fornicating, fabricating,
Conceiving lines,
Composing frameworks
(Or facades)
Recreating my figure,
My freedom,
In words

The Challenge

Dare yourself to start now;
Own the failures that may come.

Inspiration is the only
Tool you need.

The Oath
I will use my power to empathize emotion
I will use my power to express emotion
I will use my power to experience emotion
I will use my power to evoke emotion

I will.

I am...
PASSIONATE
the rose

White Flames

    A hissing, spiteful blaze,
      And fiery, fearsome flare
Whispering dangerous, foolish follies
In our unsuspecting ears.
Taking its victims hostage to a
Blind fury.

So she closes her eyes to the burning world,
Until the smoke's
      Serenading spit begs her to come closer.
The flame dances delicately, and
Holds her to his blue heart.

    She burns,
Catching the disease of the flame.
    They burn,
White and willing, while time ticks on.

(2013)

A Promise

When your tears turn to rain,
I will be your sun.
When your heart is quaking,
I will be your stable ground.
When your brain begins to erupt,
I will be your cool ocean.

You deserve
Something constant.

(2010)

Making Change
When the glass is
99% empty,
You don't focus on the fact
That it is
1% full,
You go get
more water.

The Journey
The love of this never-ending process
Might be the only thing that keeps me
writing.

Love at First Sight

When I first met him,
His hands were smaller than
My finger.

His head laid slumped against
My chest
And he slept
For hours.

Swaddled in my arms,
I learned that
Love at first sight
might be real

after all.

The Actualizer
To all the little girls who
Wanted to be
An artist, or
An actress, or
An author,
To those who lost their
Passion solely
From the insecurities
Rooted in
Comparison, or
Judgement, or
Practicality.
It's never too late
To become an
Actualizer.

I am...
POWERFUL
the tulip

Blazer
I cannot bathe in
Power so a blazer
Will have to do.

He Said, She Said
"You can't"
"Watch me."

I Decide My Titles
I tried to keep up and
Make sure I was perfect, but

I never wanted
Any of that.
Something had to change.
But you did not want
Me to start thinking for myself.

There is no happy
Medium, it's one or
The other.
Black and white

I don't change
For anyone.

(2012)

She is Strong

She holds her head so high,
Trying hard, she will not cry.
But never has to wonder why,
For strength and power don't deny
Her fearless face,
Empowered grace.

So long she's stayed within this place,
But her journey's prolonged to further space.
She will not worry,
She stands up tall
No need to hurry,
She cannot fall.

(2010)

Competition
Too many
Gain their strength from
From besting others in
Competition
When the most
Power comes from
Challenging ourselves
Beyond our
Perceptions.

Sunsets

I encourage you,
One day,
To go out
Where trees don't block
Your view,
And watch the sun
Sinking below
The horizon while
You absorb her light
Above her.

I am...
JEALOUS
the adder's tongue

Spotlights
In the darkness
we hide.

When my eyes open to bright,
I'm alone.
You're three feet away,
calling me names,
not my own.
Is this your darkness
in the light?
All these measures
Just to hide.

I cannot wait to see you
Squirm in the spotlight.

(2012)

Secondary

Green is secondary;
It is fabricated by
An artist with a brush
Dabbled in blue and
Yellow paints.

It creates a work that
Displays his own
Sadness and cowardice,
Mixing together
To reveal
Gradients with hints
Of jealousy.

Circumvent

I began to dance around the subject with distractions and art, hoping a guilty conscience would be the saving grace.

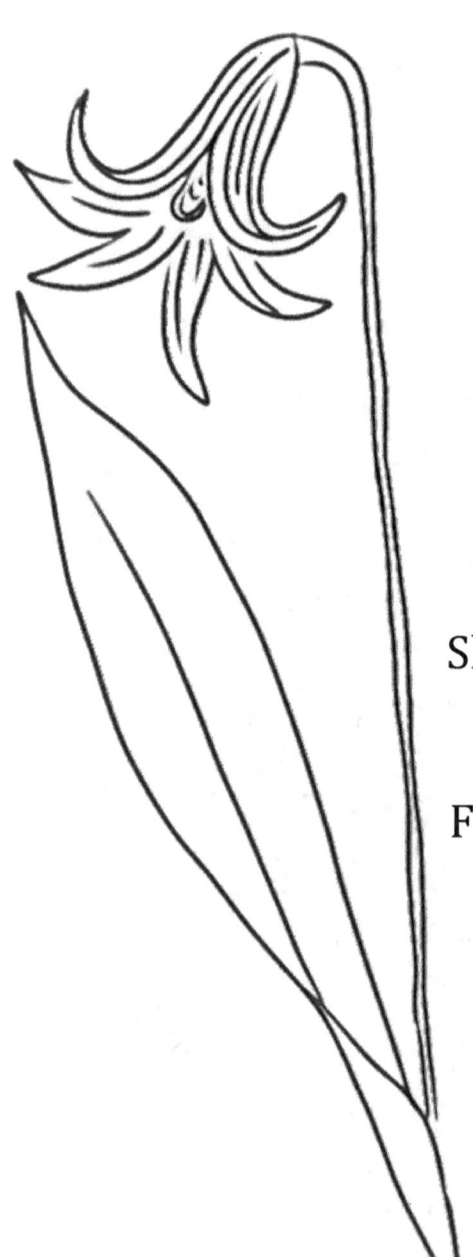

Chasing Tail
A cat that's raised
Among the dogs
Watches them try
To chase their tails.
She chases her tail too,
But she never has,
And never will,
Find the same joy in it.

Being Me
When I lost
my confidence,
I chose to write under
a false name
because being me
in my writing
was just
not good enough.

I am...
FOOLISH
the geranium

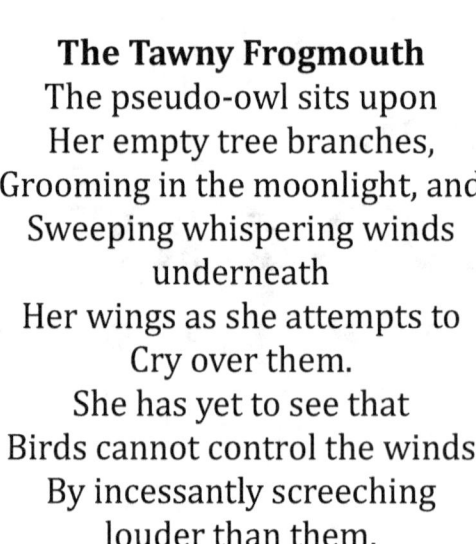

The Tawny Frogmouth
The pseudo-owl sits upon
Her empty tree branches,
Grooming in the moonlight, and
Sweeping whispering winds
underneath
Her wings as she attempts to
Cry over them.
She has yet to see that
Birds cannot control the winds
By incessantly screeching
louder than them.

Elbow

The perfect angles they make, every move intentional, every flick, hit, directly on beat. With perfectly toned frames, the angular beauties harbor sweat beyond the rough patches of skin from the wear of years and tireless effort. Now, she leaps, gracefully, forming a flawless arch, a brilliant extension, a picturesque moment. She landed on the toes of her left foot, and her weight shifted forward; all of her weight. The moment of impact, we hear the crack. Her eyes redden, her focus dead ahead.

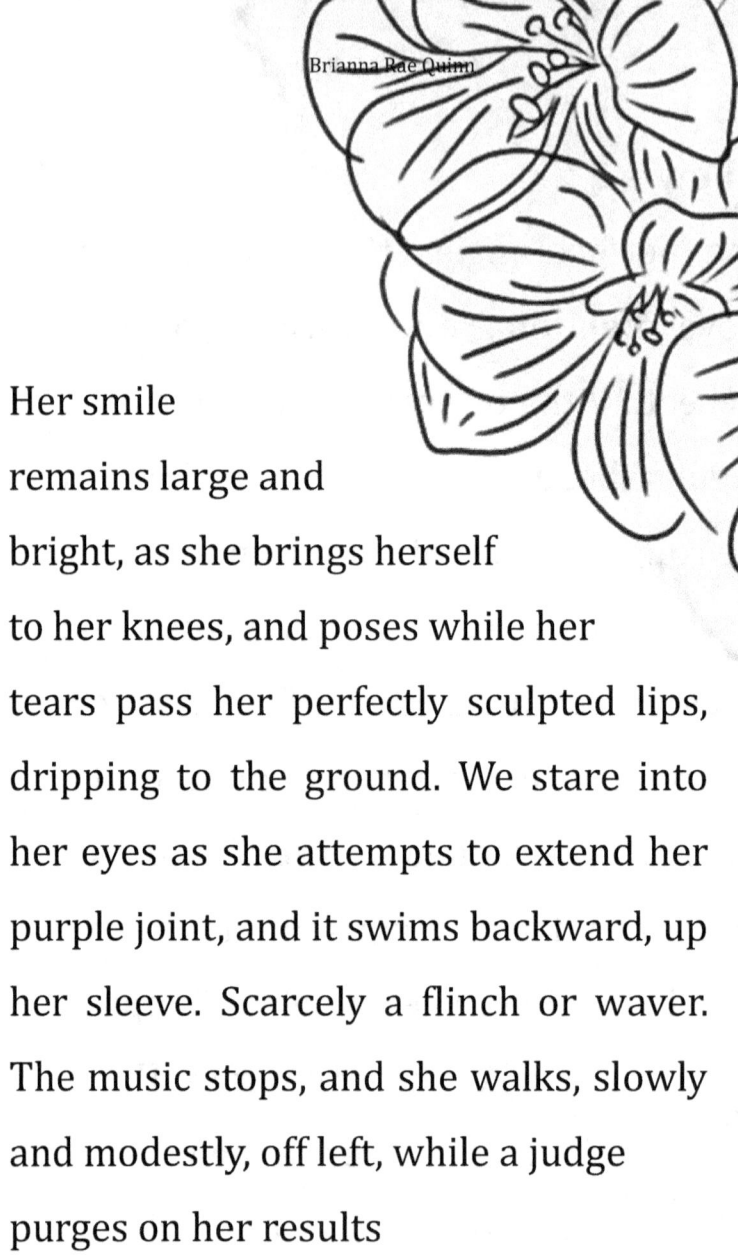

Brianna Rae Quinn

Her smile

remains large and

bright, as she brings herself

to her knees, and poses while her

tears pass her perfectly sculpted lips,

dripping to the ground. We stare into

her eyes as she attempts to extend her

purple joint, and it swims backward, up

her sleeve. Scarcely a flinch or waver.

The music stops, and she walks, slowly

and modestly, off left, while a judge

purges on her results

(2015)

Sincerely, Me

Dear the girl who writes to me,

You, whose lips had once been happy.

  Now, so foolish, lacking grace,

To feel as though nothing's left

From angry betrayal off his breath,

  And a frown that rests upon your face.

The journey's not what you'd expect,

And over him you sadly wept.

  Now, you regret each moment spent,

But with the lessons from each mistake

Soon you'll find yourself remade.

  You've learned your heart cannot be rent.

(2010)

Dicephaly
The snake with two heads
Pulls forward on two paths, but
Backward only one.

(2013)

Assumptions
The most senseless things
I've ever done came from the
fear of assumptions

I am...
AFRAID
the begonia

Safety Blanket
There are days, months, and years.
Times I've stopped thinking about it
and moments when the safety blanket extends
beyond my locked doors,

but then it comes.
That familiar sickness,
the churning in my stomach that makes it
hard to eat or to even pretend.

I can feel my eyes opening wider,
pushing beyond their natural lazy droop and
glancing in every corner,
and I'm wondering

how much money it would take
to surgically add an eyeball
to the back of my head.

Alert and frantic,
eyes peeled,
breathing, speeding,
curtains closed,

wrapped in that safety blanket
that suddenly
doesn't feel so safe,

just like another layer of clothing--
removable,
thin,
far less like armor than I wish to admit.

We've never met.
We don't need to.
I don't want to.
But since when has that
stopped you?

(2019)

Dolls
You want me to be
Still,
Unmoving
But flexible on command.

You reach out to
Close my lids,
Guide my legs.
Decide for me

What is right
Or wrong.
Stop the tears,
Smile and nod.

Stiff,
A toy
and an
Accessory,

Folded in
Your pockets,
Where you think
I'd fit so well.

Facing me
Away
So I do not know
Your intentions.

(2011)

"Come In"
When he said,
"Come in,
I did something bad,"
I hesitated.

His tone of voice,
The gravity
Made clear a violent
Truth,

And I was so afraid
Of being at the end of the knife myself,
I didn't notice the cuts
Already on his own arms.

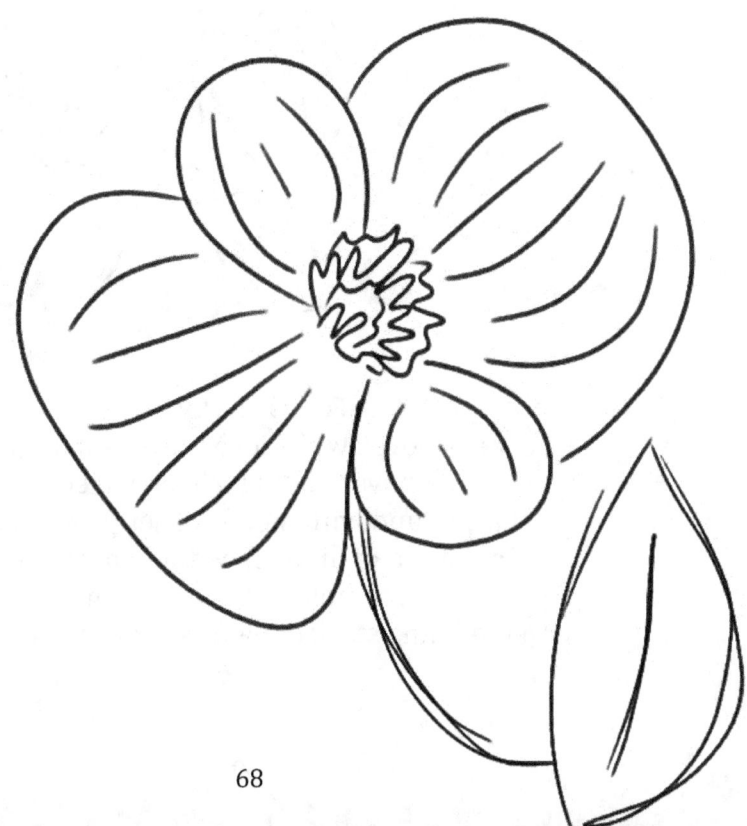

Unlocked
You didn't have to lock the door
To know you were forcing me
To open myself up and accept
You for your gratification.

You drowned me in gas,
You struck a match,
You said you needed
Payment.

You were not owed
My body, but you
Took it
Anyway.

Fear is a Novel
Fear is a novel, while love remains a fragment;
A never ending tale of hatred,
hardbound with metal corner protectors,
As a shred of unfinished thoughts fall lost,
crumpled, to the bottom
Of the piling stack of papers near the mailbox.

It Follows

Fear has pressed me into a chair,
I am frozen in unease,
with a cold breath upon my shoulder.

It whispers in my ear, daring me
To turn my head to gaze upon him.
I will not look.

Villainy takes its shape,
A beastly character,
Forcefully raising the hairs on the back of
my neck.

Even as I rise,
And start to walk away,
The hairs stay standing.

(2010)

Brianna Rae Quinn

Prey
I remember being a child
And laughing at the strange
Cars that drove back and forth
Past my driveway, nice and slow.

I posed for candid photos
For an unknown man
In his car
Without my knowledge.

I noticed strange lights from the window,
And when I pulled the curtains back
The only thing stopping that man from grabbing me
Was the wall of glass between us.

I still cannot discern as an adult
What is more terrifying to me now:
The fact that any of these things happened
Or that they just became so normal.

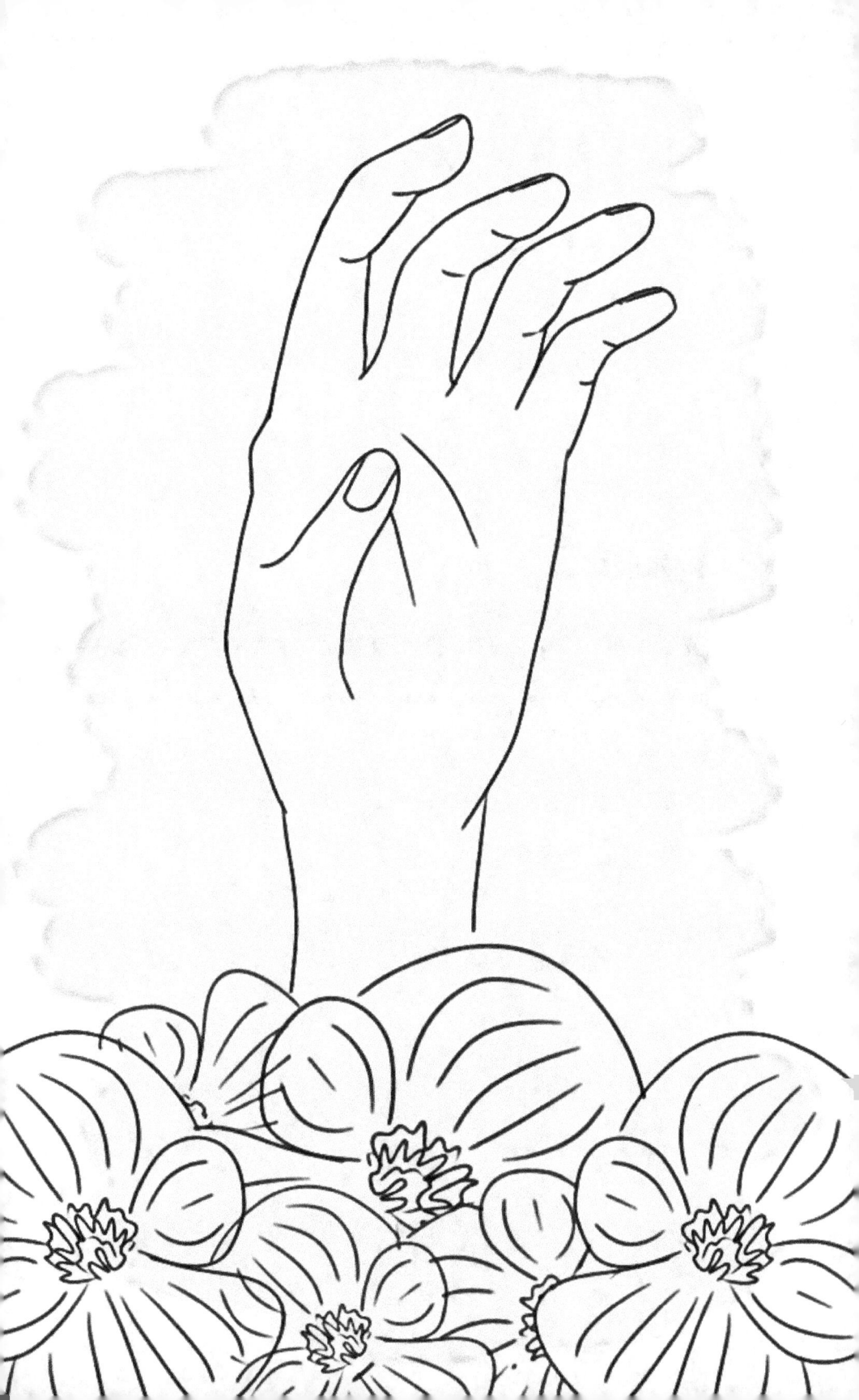

I am...
MISUNDERSTOOD
the hydrangea

Hunger
I used to say
I forgot my lunch at home.
No, I'm not hungry anyway.
I just ate a little bit ago.
I just don't like that
I'm feeling sick
My stomach just makes those noises sometimes
Mom is making something big tonight
I'm fine
Stop asking
Stop Asking
STOP ASKING

I just didn't want to think
about how hungry really I was

(2018)

Phases
The metaphorical
Moon
Often changes
Its phase
For every
Set of eyes
He encounters.

Aces
Allies have
Shown me that
Every he, she, and
Xe can learn to
Understand us
And
Let us love in peace.

Lessons

Books are not the right thing to censor.
Books are living history,
They breathe the thoughts and truths of
Times we cannot even fathom.
The pages absorb the scents
Of the worlds around them.
The spines reflect their owners'
Life-long qualities, but
The lessons stored inside
Are being lost behind
Blackened bars.

Screams
The one that
Rises from his seat
And screams
Obscenities at
The teacher
Needs the
Kindest
Possible
Response.

I am...
DEJECTED
the lily

Taking Up Space
I tried to write about you,
But the words never came.
Each phrase I tried to form,
Stayed, tangled on the tip of
my tongue.

If only words
would serve me,
Directed by the scratch
Of pencil marking,
driving you out.

Won't you occupy this space,
here on paper?
Instead of remaining
as a whisper of inspiration
in my mind.

(2010)

Unanswered

I don't ████████████████
████████████████████
████████████████████
██████████
████████████████ know
Why █████████████████
You ████ d ███ take
████████████████
████████████████████
████████████████████
████████████████ me.

Was anything real?

(2010)

Dog Tags

I remember, as a girl,
Wearing a dog collar
Around my wrist
Like a chunky bracelet.

The jingles of the tags
Prompting judging stares,
So I dropped it in my bag
Where it stayed for a few years.

This way I could
Keep my best friend
With me even after
She was gone.

By Their Count

Dust mites settle,
Absorbing water from
A cool and untouched
Wooden floor.

New salt water pools
Arrive for them each night
Before She falls asleep,

But by their count
They noticed

One less puddle today.

The Composer

He had orchestrated every rumor,
Conducting musical roars
Of hatred and disgust
When I walked into a room.

Every step I made
Was like a ping of a
Piano key in a silent space,
Drawing attention to an intruder.

He sang songs in my ears, before he
Crashed the cymbals of confession.
Instead of anger, I embraced the poor soul.
It must have been hard to be so miserable.

I am...
UNCERTAIN
the foxglove

Balance
She tried to balance
On two tight ropes. Falling to
Her imminent doom.
(2013)

Our Past
Tell me
If I say something now,
It won't erase our past.

Brianna Rae Quinn

Lying on a cloud
Lying on a cloud;
It drifts lightly along
The breeze,
Coloring everything it passes.

Lemon yellows,
Violet skies,
And eyes tracking
Feathers from the green bird
Flying around at the
mercy of the wind.

Silence fills the empty spaces after
Winds make their calls by
Gusting through the grasses,
So the sun may smile
down on her subjects.

Children, flaunting innocence,
Will join me in the clouds,
Floating on each one,
And happily trying to touch
their tongues to their noses,
As snowflakes start their rain on them.

Their eyelashes are coated,
And their laughs quiet.
Their persons turn to stone
Preparing for the coming chill.
(2009)

What If?

What ▉▉▉▉▉▉▉▉▉▉
▉▉▉▉▉▉▉▉▉▉▉▉
▉▉▉▉▉▉▉▉ if ▉▉▉▉▉
▉▉▉▉▉▉▉▉▉▉
It ▉▉▉▉▉▉▉▉
▉▉▉▉▉▉
▉▉▉▉▉▉▉▉▉▉▉
▉▉▉▉▉▉▉▉
▉▉▉▉▉▉▉▉▉
doesn't pass ▉

The Sea

In my mind there is a lonely sea.
It has no name,
But it is a part of me.

It's full of whirlpools, and deep, dark depths;
The whole is undiscovered.
Currents pull right and left.

There are so many parts;
From fish, to coral,
To the unclear water.

And the when you push yourself one way
You end up forced another.
I don't understand why it is like this.

I, the pinkest fish, must keep
My eyes open to navigate
Through green.

(2010)

I am...
CONFIDENT
the dahlia

Finding claws
I used to feel small;
I was a mouse within the walls,
And without those walls around me,
I would cower in the sun

I sat alone,
Fearing light,
Preferring darkness
To hide myself away.

I used to feel small
Comparing myself to cats,
Who needed nothing
For their defense.

I looked down at myself,
I noticed something strange,
The teeth, the fur,
The tail, the claws-- I realized

I was sitting,
Looking up to something
That wasn't quite so big
After all.

Cocky

I don't understand why others
Take the time to drag me down.

Some say confidence is key,
But some will look at me,
And say I'm cocky,

What they do not see
Is the version of me
Who took years to reflect,
And years to perfect
Another me
Who I had to reject.
I had to inspect--
I didn't respect
The me
I started to see.

Who I wanted to be
And who I was
Just didn't agree.

Then came the regrets,
Which caused the effects
I had to direct
Myself to be
A me-- happily.

If confidence is wrong,
I don't want to be right.
I've had enough of this fight
To reunite
With who I am meant to be

And If an heir of arrogance
Is the price for confidence--
I'll willfully pay that fee.

Stars
The stars don't rely
On reassurance from the
Moon; neither will I.

A Path
You go left,
I go right.
We may not meet again,
But that's okay.

An Independent Nation
I am not your colony--
You cannot take me,
You cannot change me.
without a fight.

I will kick, and I will scream,
And even if you manage
To hold me down, I know
It will not be for long.

I will rise;
I will deal the final blow.

I will take back my crown
And my independence.

Unapologetic

The dandelion
Is seen as a weed.
It invades the yards
Of unsuspecting
Suburban homes.

Gardeners will groan and
Grab the mower to shave them,
Only for their pretty yellow heads
To show up once more,
Wanting nothing
But to give you a wish.

But I don't think I could do that.
I couldn't go outside,
See a dandelion,
And shame him
For daring
To grow.

I am...
FORGIVING
the hyacinth

Forgiving
I could be
happy

It's the
fear I
will not.

(2011)

Try Again

A squirrel who jumps
from tree to tree
Cannot dwell on the
Branches he misses;
It will soon be
Winter.
He must forgive himself
And brush off the dirt to
Climb back up and
Try again
Before the snow falls.

Rumors
I'm grateful for
All the people in my life
Who have come or gone.
It's so easy
To interpret
The intentions of
Strangers with so much
Experience to go on.

Even snakes have their place
In this world.

Guilty

I never noticed that
I carried a two-ton anvil
On my back,
And left red stains
Where I shook hands.
I cannot fill the trenches
I've left, nor bleach the
Marks away, but
I can enjoy
A lighter load
By admitting
Responsibility.

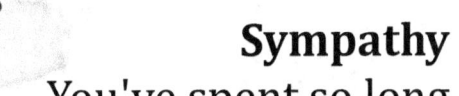

Sympathy

You've spent so long
Living a life of fantasy
To supplement the
Bore and lack of variety.

You adopted me,
A supporting character
And showed
That thrills are your priority.

So, as consolation, you only
Earned my sympathy.

I am...
ASHAMED
the peony

Broken

When I confessed,
I admitted to being different.
I told the story of a girl
Who always thought she was broken,

Who paid for powerful tools
Thinking that'd yield results,
Who sought out repairs from specialists
After practice made no difference.

When I confessed,
I admitted I was not alone
But the words in reply
Only made me feel more isolated.

I Kissed the Center of the World

I nodded at the world
As it was spinning
On an axis
And the force of gravity
Pulled down.

Your head steamed like
Molten lava
Writhing below the mantel.
You let me move the ocean,
Claiming I was the reason you went 'round.

You weren't the reason the
Earth had spun before.
Stars didn't settle in my eyes.
And meteors didn't fear you
Yanking them to the planet's core.

I turned myself away from the universe,
Orbiting your face.
I kissed the center of the world
And I managed to escape.

(2012)

Funeral

    I thought,
    They just didn't get it.
Strangers would tell me how sorry they felt, but I felt fine.
I hummed to myself to drown out the squish of the puddles beneath my feet.
I watch my young cousin, hunched over the grey mass, resting in a coffin, like a box of rocks.
He rattled the casket around with his flimsy arms.
I heard his cracking voice, screaming, "wake up!"
Clouds hung over every head but mine as
They finally set the box into the ground.
It wasn't until years later that I would realize what I was watching.
A box of every story I never heard.
All of the people in the pictures I would never know, dropped into the ground.
A piece of myself that I will never discover, surrounded in dirt and mud.
And never once did salt water flood my eyes.
And as they sobbed in each others' arms,
    They knew
    I didn't get it

(2013)

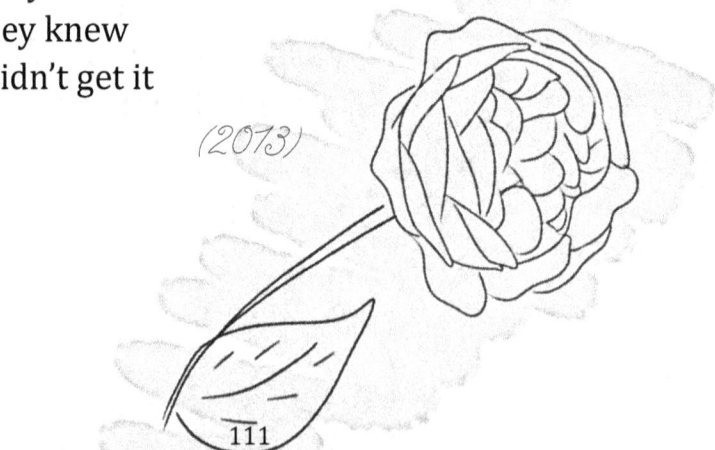

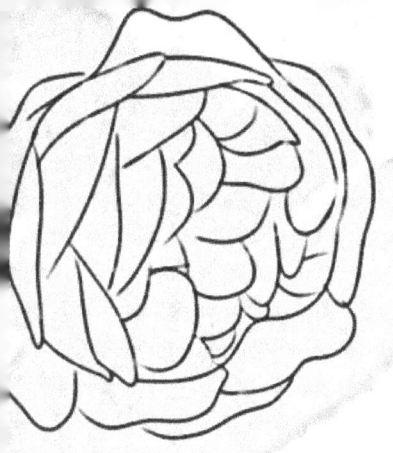

A Barcode
This box holds me in,
Graffitied with barcodes,
For easy scanning,
Identifying, and
Pricing.

Lined up on the shelves,
We are
Visually the same,
To any outside eye,
But our contents
Vary greatly.

Striped Sweaters

I wore black, grey, white,
And purple stripes
Proudly
For myself,

But when the gazes
Turned so commiserating
To my other half,
I put that sweater away.

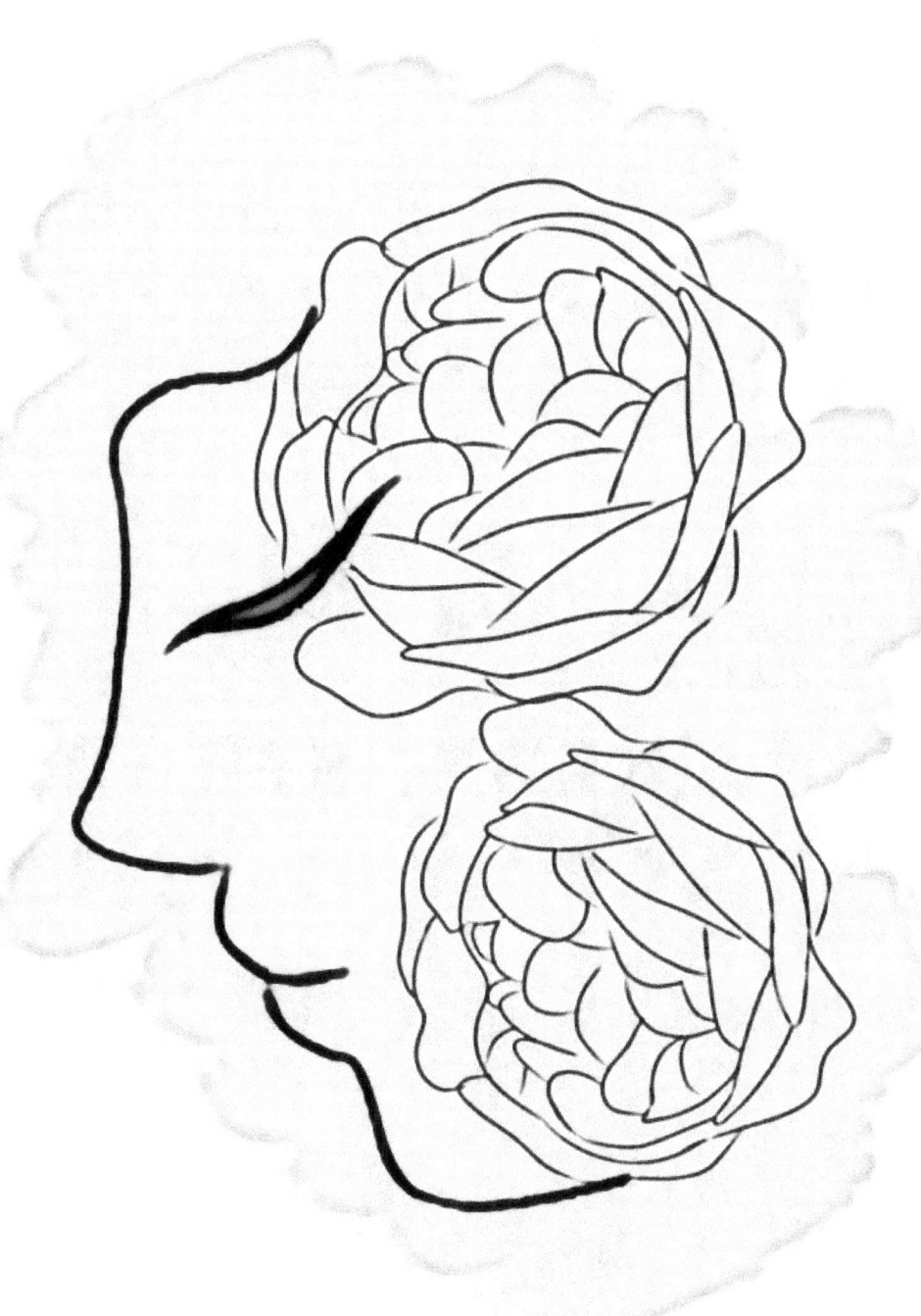

I am...
HOPEFUL
the snowdrop

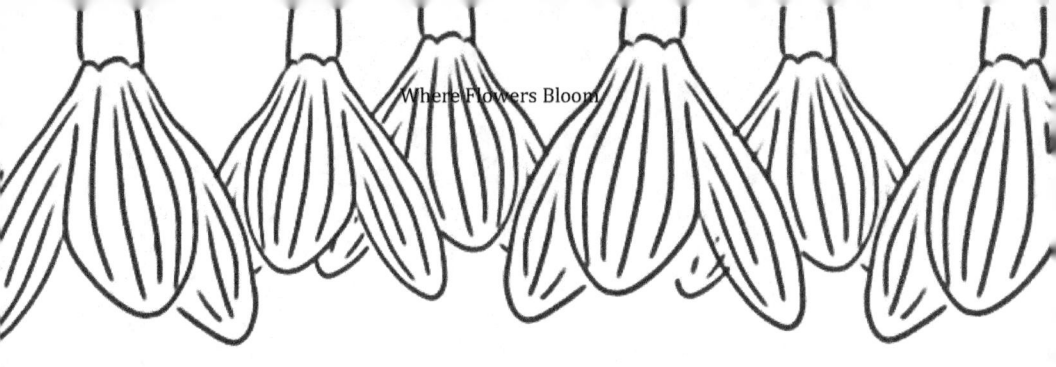

Nowhere to Go
When thunder crashes,
And lightning strikes,
The lights go out
In even the safest
Of places.

But in those
Darkest moments,
I know the storm
Will pass.
The sun has nowhere to go
But out from
Behind the clouds.

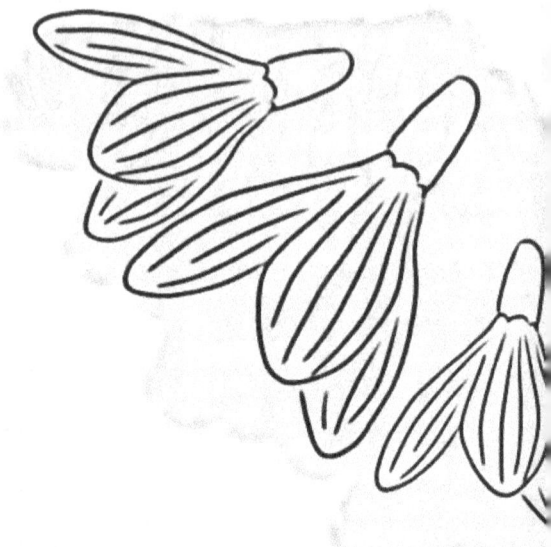

Weeded

I am a flower; and you are the caregiver to the flower bed my roots are homed.
You come out in the bright sunshine of the morning, and you see me.
You are angry; You bend down to weed the bed, and I'm the first you force out of the dirt.
My roots are strong, I will grow back.
Everyday, it's just the same.
You yank at me to remove me from your perfect garden.
I stay strong, and keep my ground.
I know someday you'll want me,
And I'll be there for you.
When you need me.

(2010)

Raven & The Dove
In a tree sits a feathered flyer.
She is dark, but hosts a heavenly glow.

"Did you see it? That Raven?
It's been flying around my head for so long."

"A Raven? No, I didn't see,
But there was a lovely, white dove."

"Impossible, there was no Dove over my head,
Only that dark Raven."

"Its possible, my friend,
That you may need a better look."

(2010)

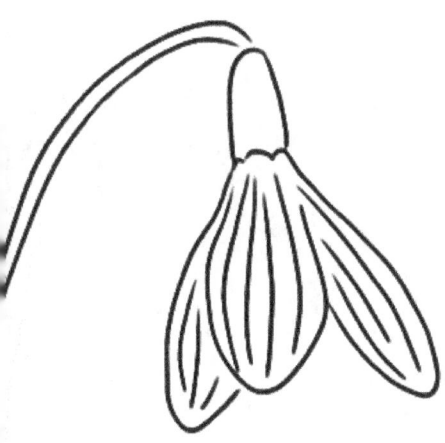

The Top of the Mountain

Frigid mountain tops
Reflect the brightest lights
And absorb every color
Into the whiteness of
The snow,
Meeting your gaze
As you take each perilous
Step on your travel
Along the cliffside.

Teacher
Even with years and miles
Between our time together,

I keep a treasure chest of
Memories strapped to my
Chest,

And I'll leave
Golden coins with
Everyone I meet

Until I have
Nothing left
To share.

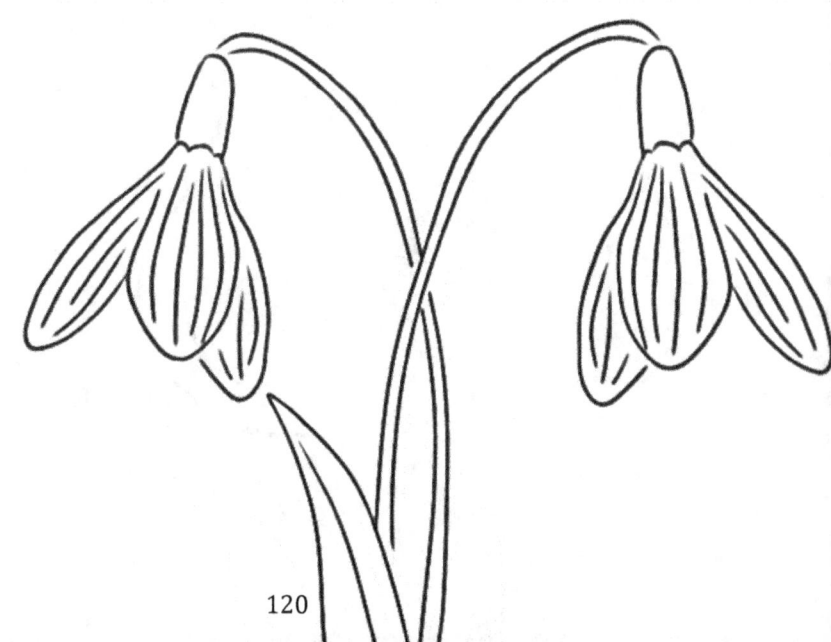

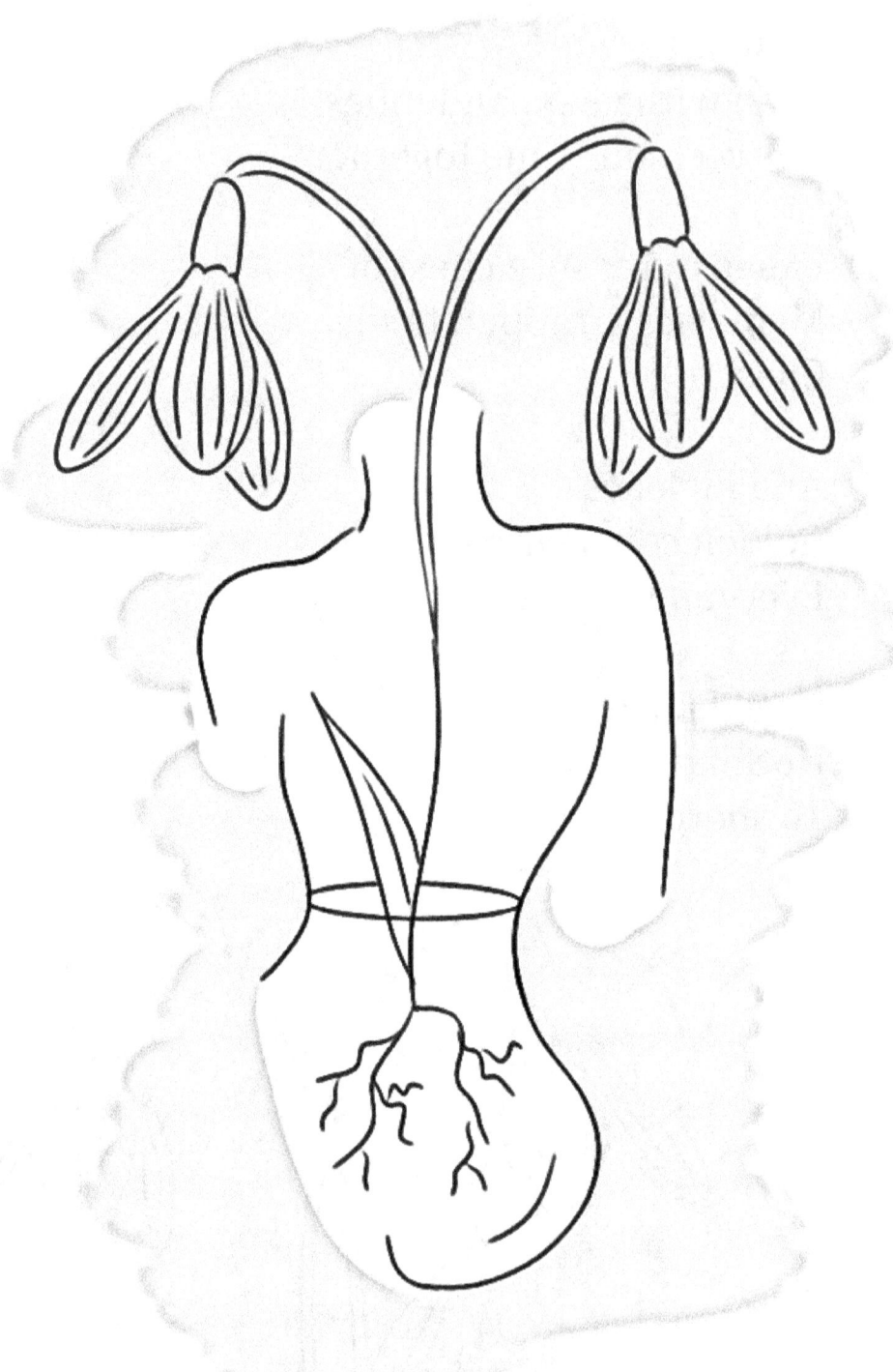

I am...
COURAGEOUS
the borage

Brianna Rae Ouinn

One Door Closed
This isn't the first time I have seen a door,
An opportunity, the one I cross often.
But I'm never sure of what lay beyond the hinges.

Each time I see a sign that says it's worth opening.
Each time it is ignored, I'm swallowed by
The disappointment of nothingness and regret.

Now, I see the door,
And another sign;
The odds are against me.

Will this risk be worth taking?
And maybe it will, but I
Will never know until I turn that handle.

One door closed, but
This time I'll keep an open mind.

(2011)

Interpretations
What if the
Pencil markings
Blend into colors
I didn't intend?
That is just a risk
I will have to take.

My Name

Letters floated in the
Hot air, filling spacing
Left around my name
From unfamiliar lips.

The atmosphere had felt
Heavy; it held me
Down and choked me
So my voice lies dormant.

The only way left,
Was to raise a blind arm and grab
The flying pieces, returning them
To my possession,

Back where it belongs.

Ivy

Ivy can only affect me
If I let myself out of the clouds.

Succulents

I admire succulents
For even in the harshest environment,
They can breach the sand.

Hurricanes

Hurricanes are
inevitable,
But it cannot stop me from
Embarking on my journey.

With a plan, and
Preparation,
I know I can
Outrun it.

I am...
TIRED
the poppy

Sunday Morning
I grabbed the stacks
Of paper and pens
And let them fall

From my hands
Into the garbage bag
I keep over my shoulder.

I shifted over, slipping on my
shoes, and stumbled into a
snowy driveway.

Did I forget to water the
plants again? Oh well,
Just another dead cactus.

(2016)

Snooze
My happiest moments,
And my most interesting
adventures are
Always cut short
By a noisy bird
In my ear,
Which loves to
Screech before
Dawn breaks and
Beg me to
Indulge in the
Mundane.

Hungry World
Trust is a part of who I am,
Still it seems the world is the lion,
and I am the lamb.

It hungers for deception,
And lies, and tears.

It tricks the lamb,
Says nothing's to fear.

So comes the end of the lamb as they know,
Though, once submitted,
They go searching for more.

(2010)

Insomnia
The brain is a gymnast
In the night, doing flips
To convince itself that it
Deserves sleep.

Popsicles
No matter how hard
You lick the popsicle's stick
Something's left behind

(2019)

Something to be Done
On my longest days,
I'll lie awake at night
Trying to mentally
exhaust myself because
Physical exhaustion isn't
Enough to ease the
Constant feelings
That something needs
To be done.

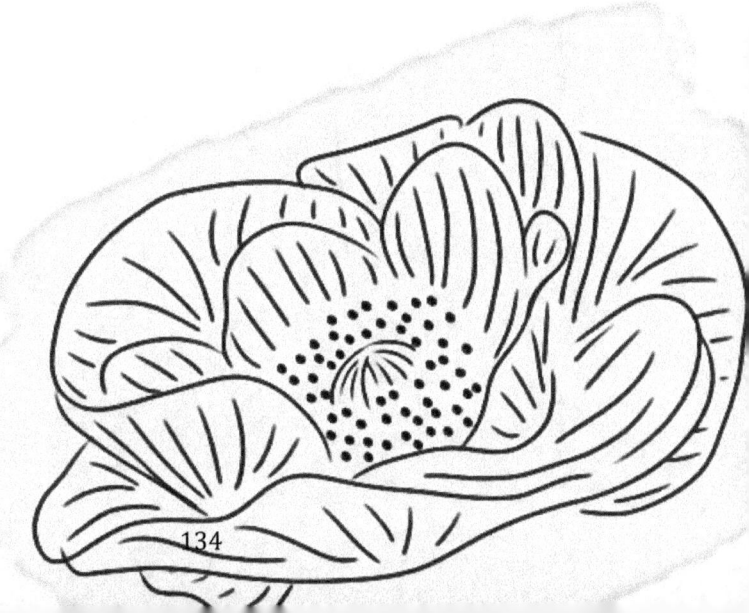

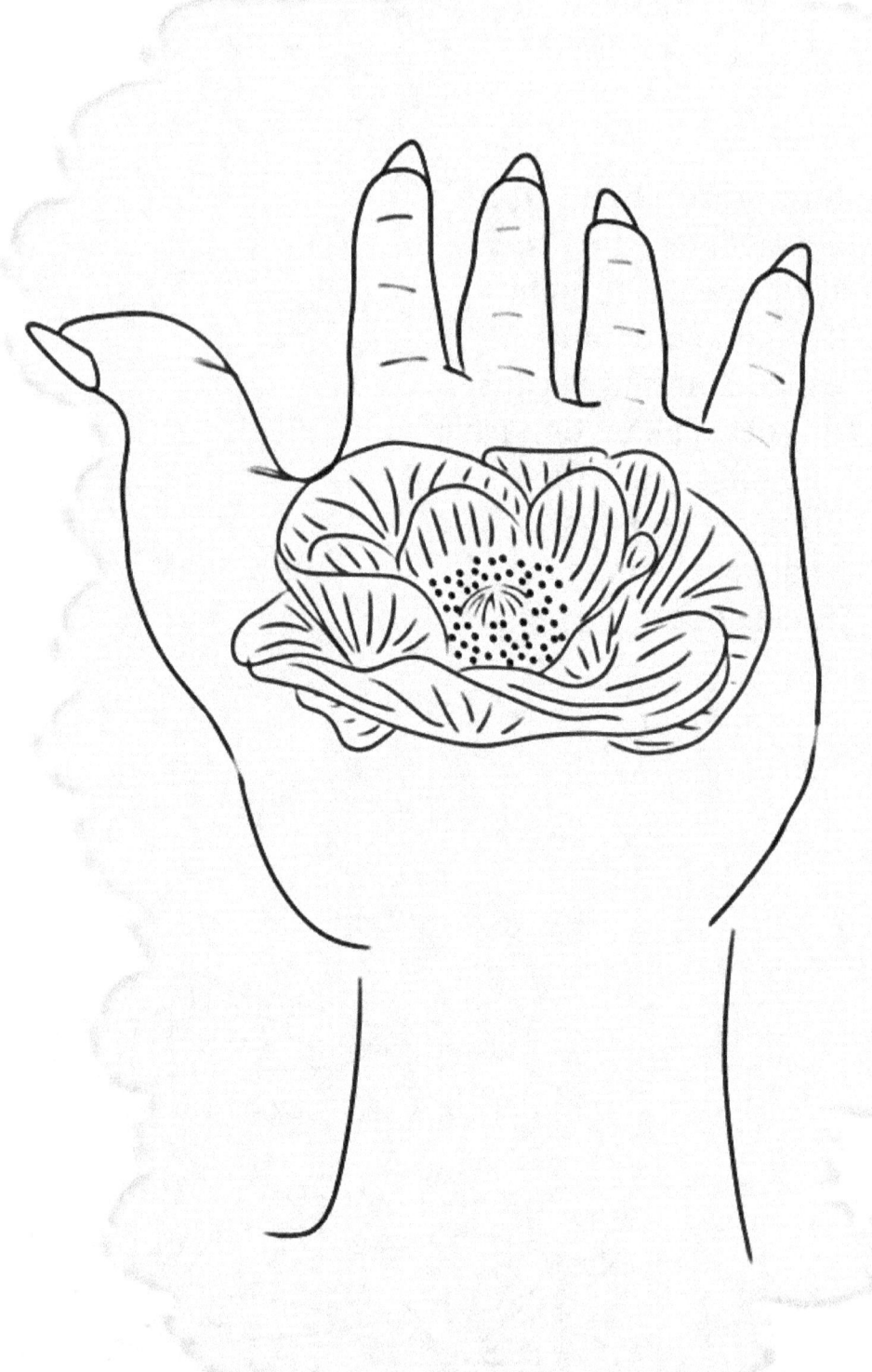

I am...
AMBITIOUS
the hollyhock

Street Lamp

Millions of people walk by.
Drunken bodies stumbling loosely over
themselves.
One man's sweat slowly slipping off
the slopes of his angular nose.

The little girl with her sunflower umbrella
skipping blissfully down the sidewalk
at her mother's side. I've never seen a live one
before. A sunflower, I mean.

When it rains like this, the bearded man
sits beneath me, collecting
raindrops in his hands,
hoping he can once again observe

his skin, shown under the light.
We often collect dust together and
stare at the skyscrapers,
picturing how different our lives would be

if we worked inside.

(2015)

Flying
I'd rather jump and fall
Than to be able to fly and never know it.

Fourteen More
Every day I write
One thousand words, but only
Ten will stay in place.

Brianna Rae Quinn

Rooted
I started growing
Toward the sun
As soon as I
Could feel it,

But I'll always
Stay rooted
In this same
Old pot.

The Steepest Staircase

Climbing a staircase is
never easy;

The flight that
Reaches highest
Has tons of
Tiny jumps,

And the fewest steps
To the top will
Keep you lowest
To the ground.

Steps
I am allowed
To take steps
In the wrong
Direction
As long
As I never
Let myself
Stop
Moving.

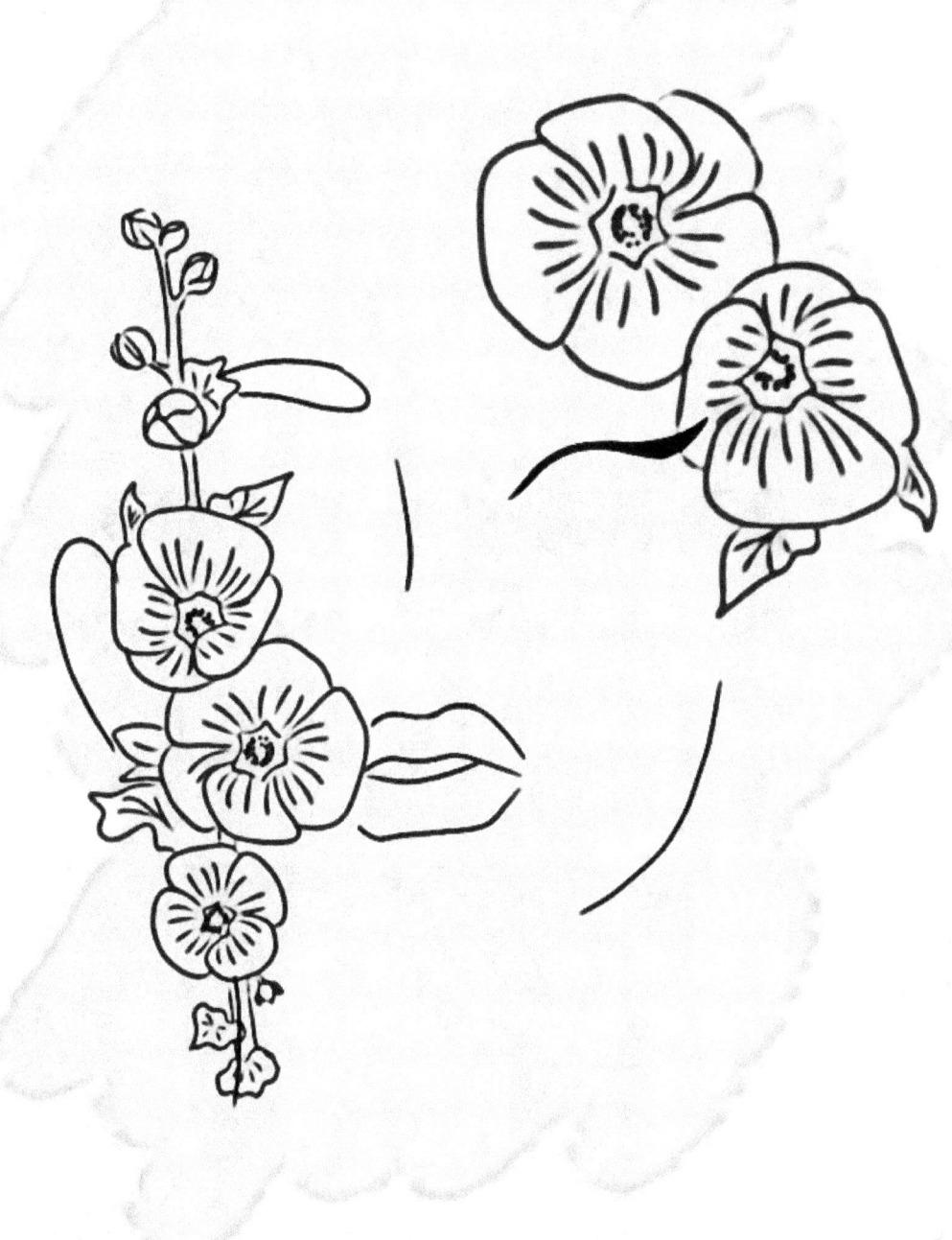

I am...
PROUD
the amaryllis

Glittering Memories
To my sisters,
And to the survivors.
To those who have overcome,
And those who are still trying.

I see the jewels upon your crown,
Homing private, painful memories
Of the many times you must have looked
A challenge in the eye.

They adorn your head to be admired,
Whether or not you know.

Solid Victory

Salted drops drip into your mouth,
Horrid odors reach for your nose
Reaping their way through your senses.
Jealous hands are magnetized to each other,
Compelled by the duty of civility--
A harsh, rasping roar.
You're freezing and burning at the same time;
a steaming frost, like dry ice.
Your chest pounds against your skin.
You can feel it bruising.

A glittering reflection faces you, sweat beading
from the hairline.
It seems beaten-- dead,
Worked until it couldn't,
But still housing a smile, emanating pride.

This was your struggle,
This was your fight, and
In shaking hands you hold
A solid victory

(2012)

Feathers

The peacock splays his train out wide,
Shaking loose for all to see.
He notes each feather has a name,
And a story for each eye.

Recognition, milestones,
Boasted proudly on display,
But his favorites hold the tales
That only he will know.

Feathers fall as others grow
In shades of blue and green,
And even when he drops his tail,
Those feathers follow close behind

No
I was the girl
Who changed the date of her birthday
So it would work better for my
Friends.

I was the girl
Who left her phone on all night
To be a taxi service for a former
Bully and his brother.

I was the girl
Who heard, "I'll pay you back", and over-
drafted
Her account to pay a tow truck for her
lover,

And that first day
I said the word "No"
Was one of the proudest days
Of my life.

A Decade Later
Flipping through the pictures
In a photo box under my
Bed I saw a photo of
A girl whose wistful eyes seemed
To search for something never to come.

I noticed little things, like her dark clothes
to feel skinny
The hair in her face to hide what she didn't
think was pretty,
And a wide smile under those lying, longing
eyes.

Even still, I did not pity her,
She's on a journey to find herself.
So I taped her photo on the mirror
To let her see the incredible woman
She would be one day.

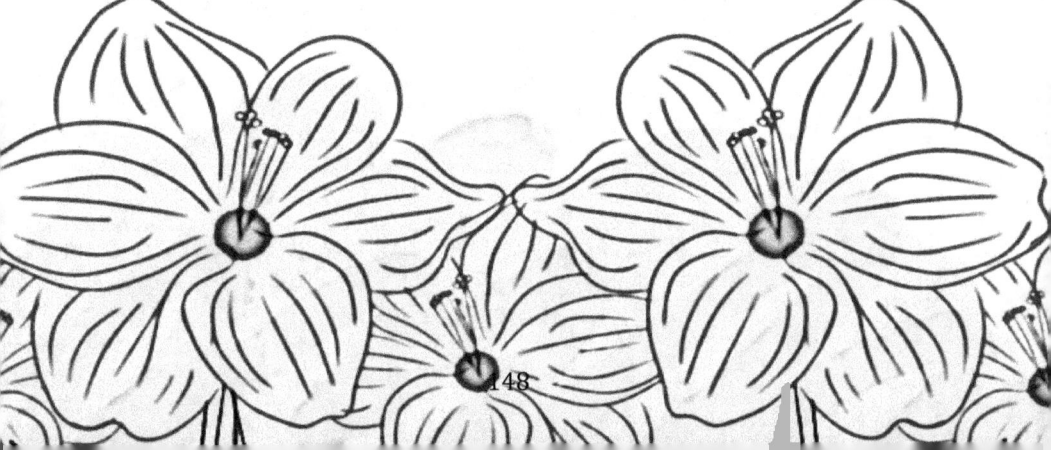

I am...
AT PEACE
the lavender

If the Winds Could Speak
If the winds could speak,
They'd remind you of the past
And whisper stories from across the world.

They'd sit in your old rocking chair
And kick their legs until you sit to listen,
All the while making the old wood creak.

They would race you in your car
When you had your windows down
And taunt you once they won.

They would blow you back inside
In the morning, so you'd have at least
One moment to yourself.

Take My Rain

Like a solemn elder bird,
You spoke wisdom in every word.

Always a clear, bright blue sky
Bringing comfort to the greyest cloud's cry,

And that kindness, it makes me wonder
Why you challenge each roll of thunder.

You take my rain and send
It down the river,
And around each bend
It leaves forever.

(2012)

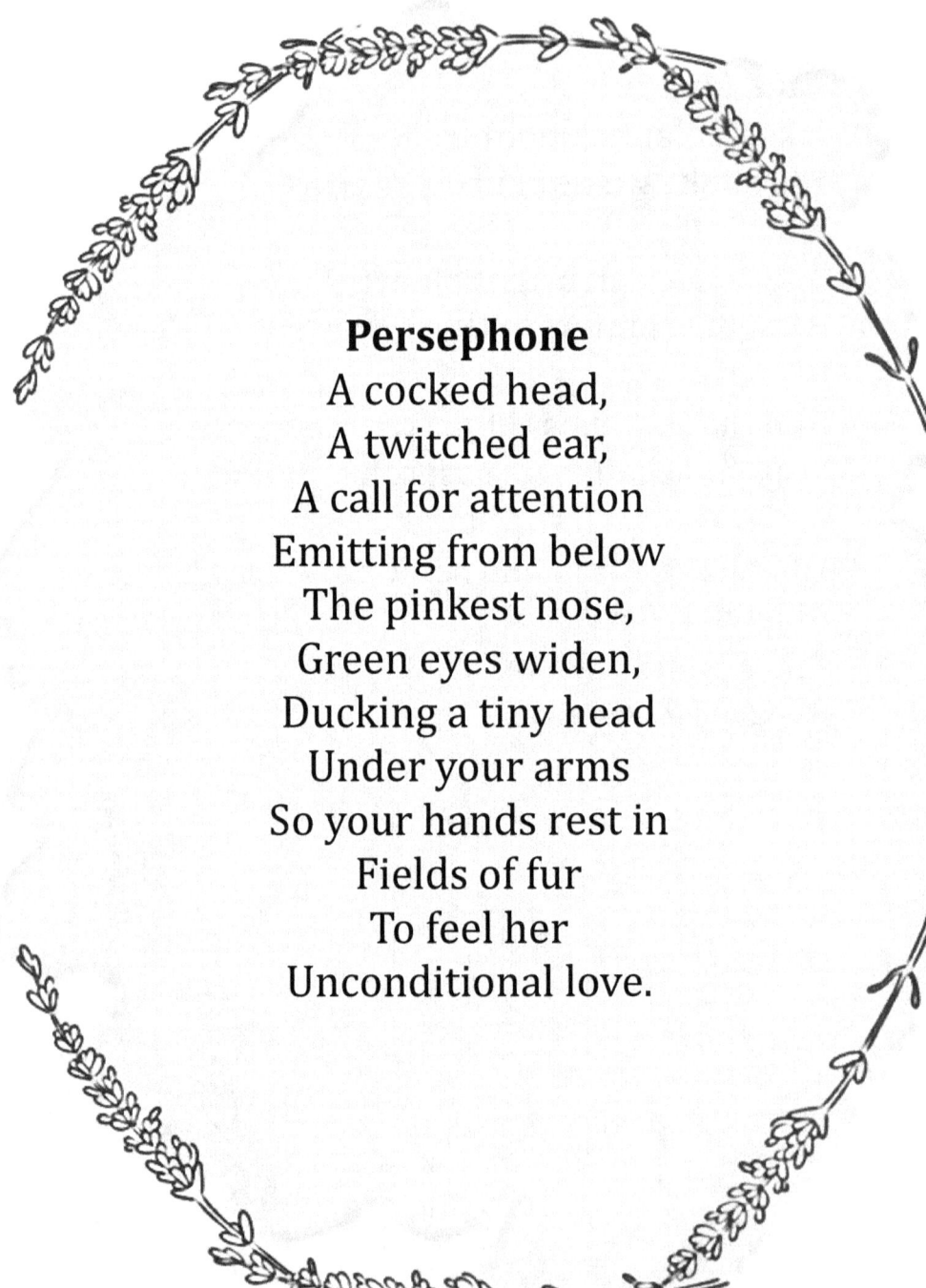

Persephone

A cocked head,
A twitched ear,
A call for attention
Emitting from below
The pinkest nose,
Green eyes widen,
Ducking a tiny head
Under your arms
So your hands rest in
Fields of fur
To feel her
Unconditional love.

Tea
Gentle steam rising steady
From her mouth, she readies for
A journey through a tunnel
To a cave that's deep below,
Where she hugs against the walls
To hope her warmth
Will bring you peace
from the inside out.

Libraries in Winter
The smell of libraries
In winter time
Smells, to me, like
Potential
For a cozy trip
Through fantasy worlds
And haunted homes.
How else can one
Be at a beach
And still see untouched
Virgin snow by only
Looking left?

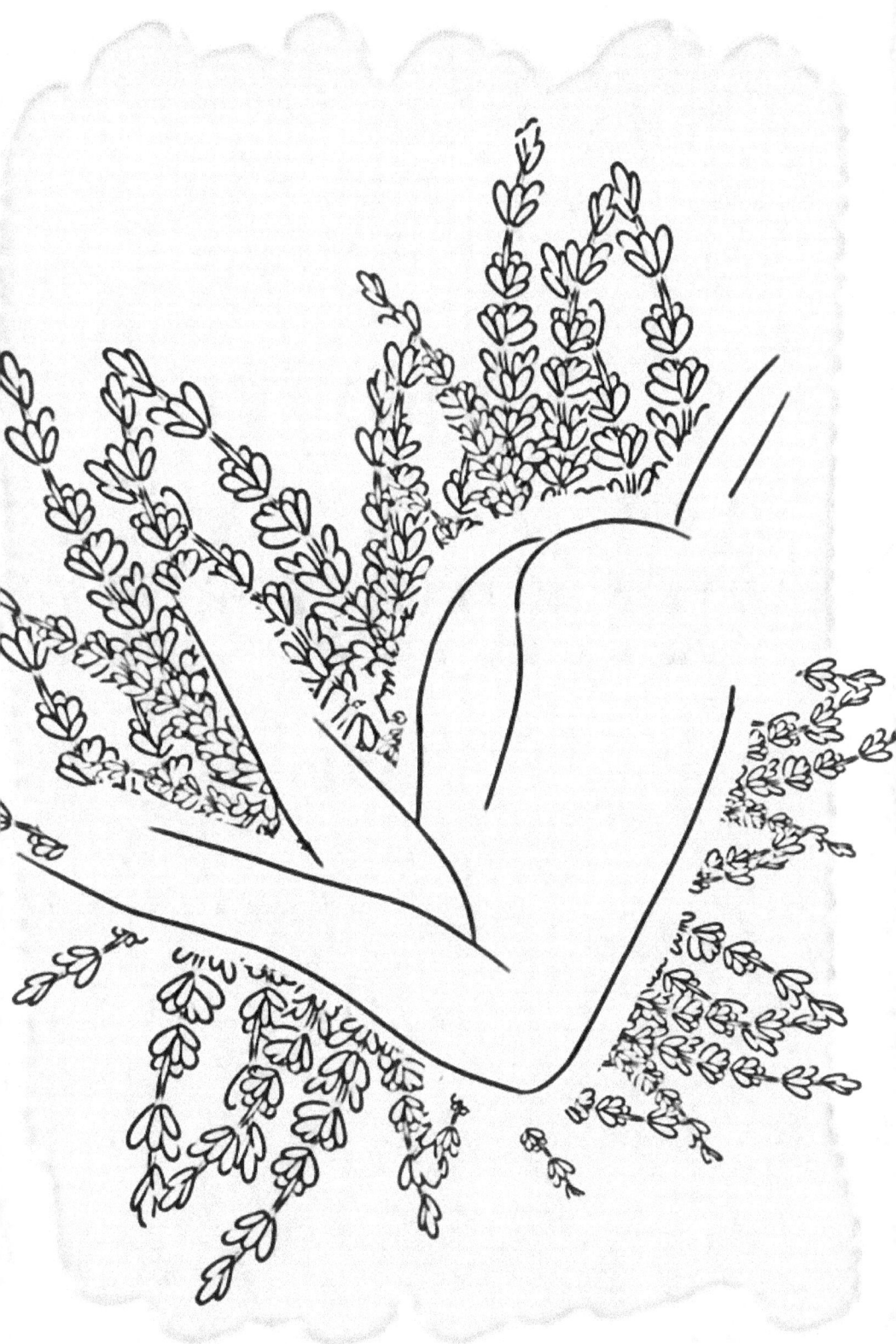

I am...
THANKFUL
the sweetpea

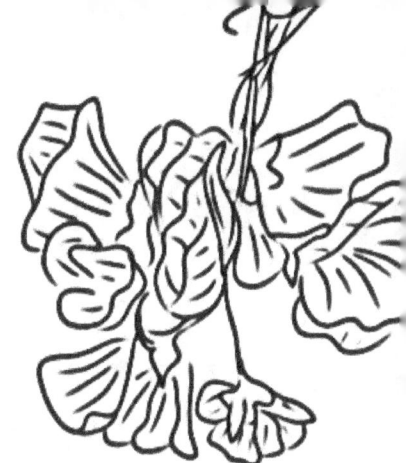

The Final Letter
Dear Reader,
After a decade of writing
and self-discovery,
I must thank
every person
who has found themselves
amongst these pages.

Those of you
that braved this journey
with me
have given these words
more meaning
than I ever could.

Sincerely,
Brianna Rae

Acknowledgements

I'd like to thank several people for helping me get to this point, starting first and foremost with my best friend and first Beta Reader, Chrissy Margevicius. She's seen me write and grow through the majority of the texts in this book. She's helped me grow as a person and an artist, and has been my go-to for everything, big and small, in the past decade. A big part of who I am now is thanks to her and her support.

I'd also like to thank Nicholas Kemper, both my biggest critic and my biggest supporter. He'd do anything for me, even if it means telling me my word choice is terrible. His honesty and patience with me really made this book the best it could be.

Of course, I'd like to thank everyone who was so supportive of my announcement and let me talk about the writing process basically non-stop for weeks, no matter how vaguely; Shelby Dodds, Ben Essex, Morgan Phillips, Miranda Mariner, Madeline Sleeper, and Jeremy Smith.

Next, I'd like to thank a collection of seemingly random names, most of whom I have not spoken to in years, some of whom I am no longer on good terms with, but ten years ago, on July 21 of 2010, I put a status on my Facebook page asking my friends to like the status if anyone thought it would be a good idea for me to write a poetry book. The following people liked the status and probably unknowingly managed to push me to this point: Katherine Tekesky, Matthew Mysliwiec, Rebecca Hu, Penny Kmitt, Caitlin Albright, Ally Deal, Alyssa Herbell, Jessica Babka, and Karen Grasso. I hope this doesn't put any undue pressure on you to actually read the book!

And lastly, Mr. Hemery, my creative writing teacher from 2012; I hope I've grown enough as a writer to make you proud.

Thank you all, once again, for helping this life-long dream of mine become a reality. I am eternally grateful.

Brianna Rae Quinn

www.ingramcontent.com/pod-product-compliance
Lightning Source LLC
Chambersburg PA
CBHW072158100526
44589CB00015B/2280